Piano/Vocal

Ben Folds So There

Cover and "F10-D-A" illustrations by Alex Sopp

Master Recordings ℗ New West Records. Used by permission.

To access audio visit:
www.halleonard.com/mylibrary

Enter Code
4025-2533-7640-5673

ISBN 978-1-5400-1167-1

7777 W. BLUEMOUND RD. P.O. BOX 13819 MILWAUKEE, WI 53213

In Australia Contact:
Hal Leonard Australia Pty. Ltd.
4 Lentara Court
Cheltenham, Victoria, 3192 Australia
Email: ausadmin@halleonard.com.au

Visit Hal Leonard Online at
www.halleonard.com

Some of my stuff is easy to play. Some not quite so easy. My goal was to transcribe these songs in a way that relays what I would ideally play. That said, each time I play a song, I do it a little differently. These scores are for solo piano and voice. The album *So There* was recorded with a six-piece chamber ensemble (yMusic), and my piano was reduced to fit into those arrangements. So, in a way, some of this may be more difficult than what you hear on the studio record.

Included are recordings of me sitting down at the piano and singing some of these songs. You'll notice quite a few differences between what's written and what's being played. I think that's the nature of rock and roll — being in the moment. Especially "Yes Man," where on this particular performance I ignored much of what I wrote. It's just how I played it that once. Oh well.

Once you've learned these songs the way I've written them, I'd encourage you to stray, if that's what you're feeling. In other words, these shouldn't be played precisely, even though they're specific. When it's time to perform something, for yourself or an audience, you just have to go for it. No pussyfooting around anymore. In performance, you might stumble your way over something that should have been carefully articulated. That's not ideal, but it's better to mean it, to express. It's always amazing how much detail we get right when our intention is to communicate. Neither the composer, performer, nor the audience was ever served by a tentative or sterile performance that overlooked the story of the music while accomplishing the tasks of phrases as if ticking off answers on a test.

So! Practice until you're blue in the face and try like hell to get it all right. That's what I do. But do what it takes to get the point across with abandon when performing. This is the spirit in which I've written these piano parts for this book. I hope this helps students in some way for any kind of music. (But don't tell your teacher that came from me!)

A few idiosyncratic techniques of mine you're welcome to apply to these songs:

Feet — on floor, and on the pedal as percussion. I couldn't have done years of solo performances without my secret percussionist attached to my shins. Maybe it's because I was a drummer, or maybe it's because I've had to fill the sound that a band normally does. We're taught not to stomp around, but hey, we were never told to grunt and hum and that certainly didn't stop Glenn Gould or Keith Jarrett gurgling over the music like pirates. Keeping time and making sounds feels good sometimes, so feel free to wear the floor, the pedal, and your glottis out. I often slam the sustain pedal hard with my right foot on beats two and four of a section that needs more groove. I've notated some of these moments. It gives you some thump, as well as an undercurrent of reverb which reinforces that groove. Use sparingly as this gets old quickly.

Normally when using the damper pedal, my preferred technique is what's known as "delayed pedal" — applying the damper just after you play the note or chord. I can use it liberally that way without smearing over the phrases too much. I don't really use the damper pedal before or with the notes very often. That's just me. I also use the sostenuto pedal sometimes, which I've indicated in the music. It's helpful for the same reason — getting sustain without smear, so you can articulate freely with both hands up the keyboard while bass notes sustain like cellos beneath it all.

On loud bursts of chords — sort of a piano version of a "power chord" — no matter how short, I like to kick the damper pedal so hard it reverberates all the strings of the piano. That adds color and violence I couldn't get otherwise. I always apply this when I smash clusters of random notes in the bass, like thunder. I've notated those as "palm clusters" or "forearm smashes." Feel free to add delayed pedal to those bombs and never mind the recovery time of the piano into the next phrase. Hear it as smoke clearing. It's good drama!

– Ben Folds

CAPABLE OF ANYTHING

Words and Music by
BEN FOLDS

Workout Video Tempo (♩ = 160)

Verse

What is ___ this? _

Dynamics/pedaling meant to imitate delay effect in two-bar sets -----

It does-n't make much _ sense. _ They sing it like a

NOT A FAN

Words and Music by
BEN FOLDS

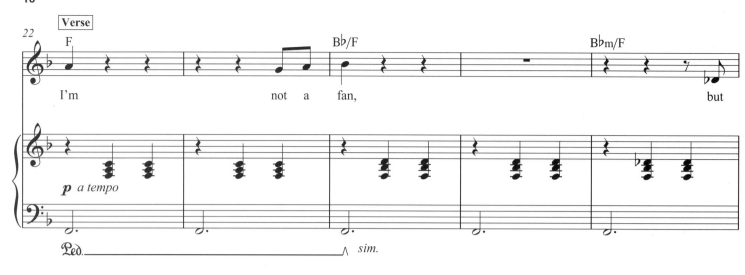

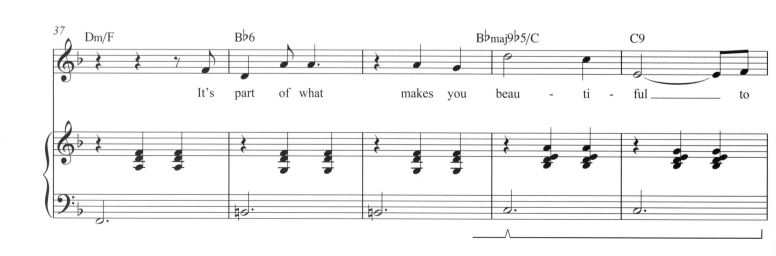

I'll be third wheel. So go get your t-shirt signed,

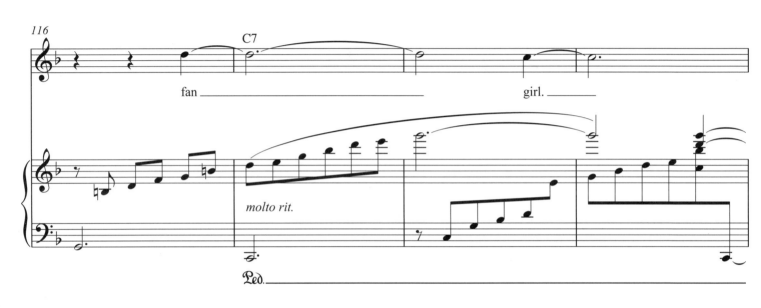

fan _____ girl. _____

Rubato   **Tempo primo (♩ = 140)**

I may, or may not be here when you re-turn.

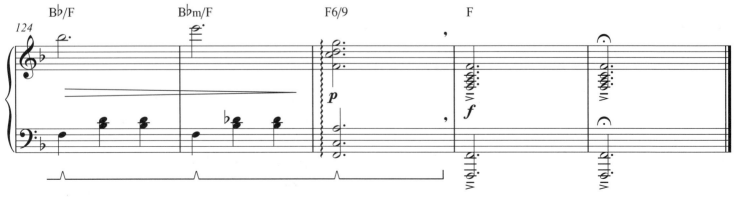

SO THERE

Words and Music by
BEN FOLDS

Note: Accenting beats 2 and 4 are essential to the feel of this song.
Delayed pedaling for duration on those beats helps the groove.

mat - tress and ___ a ster - e - o ___

Verse

Through shin - y streets __ and dirt - y snow __ blue skies __ in Dit - mas __ Oh Brook-lyn it's __ my

LONG WAY TO GO

Words and Music by
BEN FOLDS

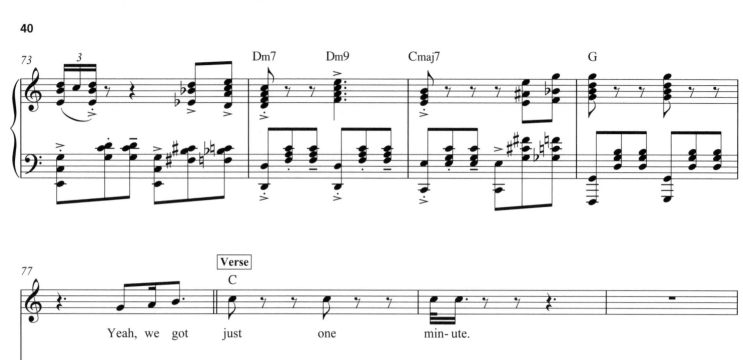

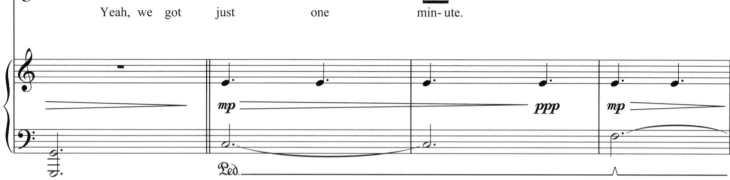

Yeah, we got just one min-ute.

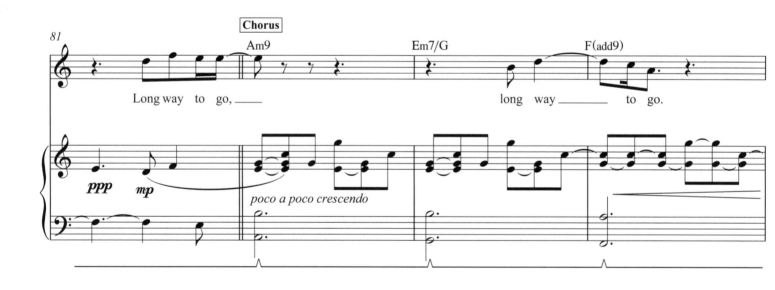

Long way to go, ____ long way ____ to go.

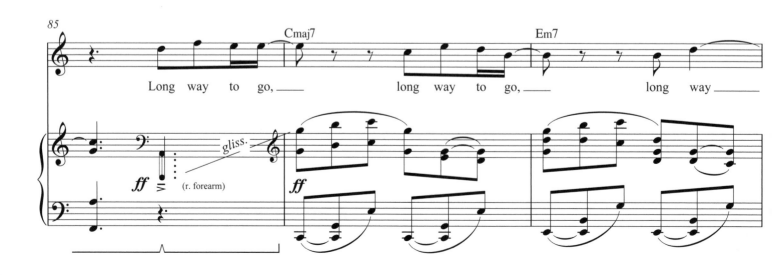

Long way to go, ____ long way to go, ____ long way ____

PHONE IN A POOL

Words and Music by
BEN FOLDS

Drunk, But Steady ($\quarternote = 99$)

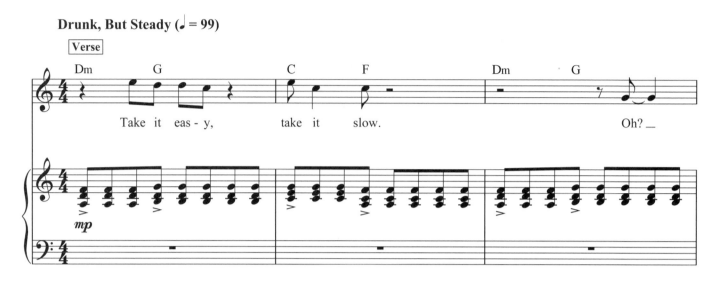

Take it eas-y, take it slow. Oh? __

Get on __ with the show oh, that's what I

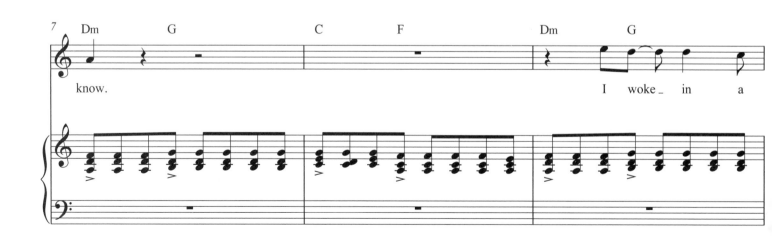

know. I woke __ in a

YES MAN

Words and Music by BEN FOLDS
and ROB MOOSE

Why did-n't you tell me that I got fat? It's so eas-

y I can see it now I'm look-ing back, as I emp-ty one __ more round __

"F10-D-A"

Did you know that each note of the piano is named after the letters of the alphabet?

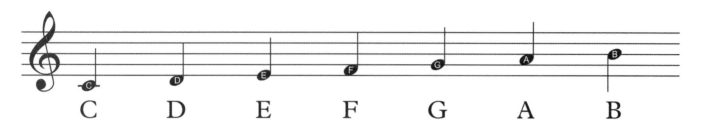

And did you know that some letters, when spoken, also sound like a **whole word?**

And did you know that some words are **so bad** that when spoken on TV you're only allowed to use the first letter of that word?

Let's sing these notes and see what they mean to your friends when they hear them!

"F!"

"F *10* D A!"

"*with* A D"

"A *big fat* D"

"C - E *what it's like to* B"

"F *10* D A!"

"*oh* G*eee!*"

I'M NOT THE MAN

Words and Music by BEN FOLDS
and ALICIA WITT

Note: Use a delayed damper pedal
liberally throughout.

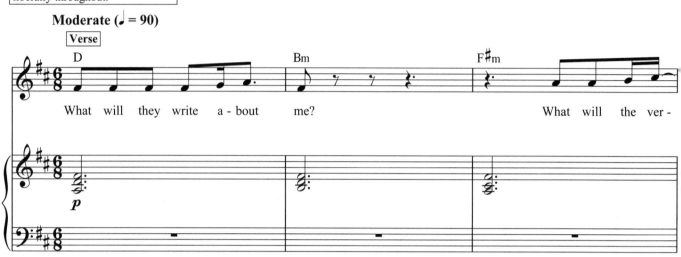

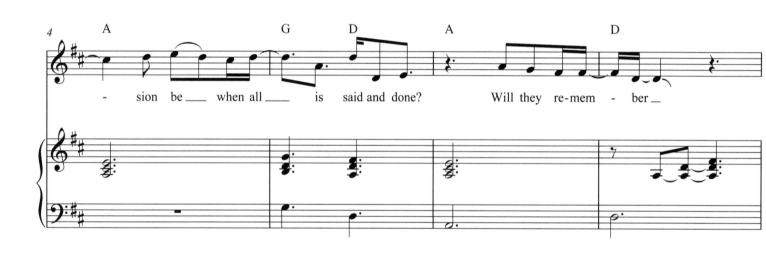

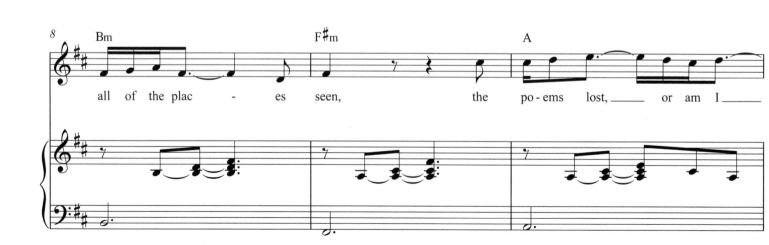